To Patricia Foster with gratitude!

Copyright © 2014 by Tijuana Boswell

All rights reserved. No part of this publication may be reproduced or transmitted in any form or by any means, electronic or mechanical, including photocopy, recording, or any information storage and retrieval system, without permission in writing from the copyright owner.

ISBN-13: 978-1502935762

ISBN-10: 1502935767

"Men Are Not the Only Dogs!" is registered at the WGA #1752953

Library of Congress # TX8-216-644

Printed in the United States of America

INTRODUCTION

This is a dramatic fictional novel written to inform individuals to be grateful for their accomplishments. And to not allow greed, revenge and covetousness destroy their prolific lifestyles and honorable character.

TABLE OF CONTENTS

Chapter	Page
"She's So Greedy"	5
"She's Game"	11
"A Fibbing Whore"	14
"A Strumpet Trains"	17
"No Free Ride"	22
"Can't Judge A Whore"	26
"A Secret Admirer"	30
"Flea Powder, Please!"	33
"That Girl Is on Fire"	40
"A Lot of Freaking Going on"	44
"Little Sis Caters"	51
"Somebody's Watching"	57

TABLE OF CONTENTS (ctd)

Chapter	Page
"Who's Crazy?"	68
"Finally! A Committed Whore"	73
"A Courtesan Out of Business"	76
"She's Living Her Dream"	81

"SHE'S SO GREEDY"

Chicago, Illinois

A mailman walks down a cobblestoned driveway with a curb appeal to a two-story, high-priced home. It has a large backyard with a swimming pool and located in an upscale neighborhood, where only the elite reside. He rings the doorbell then Ramone Hampton, a 35-year-old, very rich music promoter for Preeminent Records answers the door.

The mailman hands him a small package. Ramone signs for it then closes the door. Ramone opens the parcel and extracts a men's diamond Rolex watch.

His gorgeous 30-year-old wife, Yasmine Hampton is placing breakfast on the table for him, her and their lovely 8-year-old daughter, Deja Hampton.

"That's too big for me." Yasmine jokes about the watch.

"My new artist is going to love this signing gift." Ramone says.

"He should." Yasmine says.

"Daddy I want to be a singer. Will you sign me?" Deja ask with mouthful of syrupy pancakes.

"When you're grown." Ramone replies, taking a seat at the table.

Deja pouts.

After breakfast, Ramone grabs his briefcase, kisses his family then exits the house to work. Yasmine removes the dirty dishes from the table and places them in the sink then grabs her purse. Deja grabs her backpack then they exit the house en route to school.

They arrive then Deja kisses her mother and exits the vehicle and enters the school. Yasmine take off to work at "Le Meilleur Gym", where she's a fitness instructor. She arrives and exits her vehicle sporting her workout gear that shows off her large butt, 32b sized breast, 24-inch waist and bowlegs.

Male construction workers at a nearby work site cat call and whistles at her. Yasmine smiles, waves her hand at them then enters the gym. She begins to work out with a client.

After 4 hours has passed, it's lunch time. So, Yasmine dials her 25-year-old step sister, Lenelle Asperson. She's single, childless and moderately attractive. She's a 911 operator by night and part-time nursing student by day.

Lenelle has a mediocre body and a trustworthy spirit. She's dating a stingy psychiatrist named Osai Ingram. He's a 31-year-old, childless, single and handsome guy.

Osai owns several offices in which one is located in the neighborhood where he resides. He's really not into Lenelle because she doesn't give him sex. So, he lies by saying he sometimes has clients at his home during lunch, as an excuse to not be with Lenelle.

Lenelle and Osai live separately in a condo building that's close to many restaurants and walking distance from Yasmine's job.

Lenelle's phone ring.

"Hey girl." Lenelle answers.

"It's chow time for me. Do you want to join me for Chinese?" Yasmine asks.

"Sounds good." Lenelle replies.

"Meet me at the restaurant in ten minutes." Yasmine says, then ends call.

Later, they arrive at the restaurant and order their food then begin to converse while waiting. Yasmine comments that she wants a new Porsche.

"What's wrong with your BMW?" Lenelle ask.

"Nothing. I just want a second car…I am keeping my BMW." Yasmine replies, greedily.

"Your three thousand dollar a month allowance from yo' hubby and your decent paying job, should get it." Lenelle states.

"I only spend my money on clothes, nails, hair and my daughter…not on expensive bills." Yasmine says, selfishly.

      Lenelle complains that Osai doesn't give her money and she needs help with her student loans. Yasmine suggest that she give him sex. Lenelle refuses because he hasn't proven he's worth it.

She wants him to provide her with support before she gives in to him.

"Y'all been dating for six months and you still haven't set it out…not even a little head! Why are you with him?" Yasmine asks.

"We rarely date. Hell, he works through his lunch, instead of hanging out with me. I do like him and I guess the idea of having a doctor for a boyfriend, fascinates me and keeps me around." Lenelle replies, immaturely.

"Do not look at his title, but his heart." Yasmine preaches.

"As long as my wallet is empty, he won't even be allowed to smell it." Lenelle says, stubbornly. "I asked him to give me three hundred dollars for books. He told me to repay him in two weeks." Lenelle complains.

"Maybe he knows you are with him for his status." Yasmine accuses.

"That's not true…I care about him! He's just stingy as hell!" Lenelle responds, defensive.

"You are smart enough to get the dollars up front…I praise you for that." Yasmine says, surprised.

The waiter brings their beverages.

"Let him go." Yasmine advises.

"I'm seriously thinking about it. I may not have a body like yours, but my big boobs and legs do turn heads…they turned his." Lenelle brags.

"Then put them to work." Yasmine instructs, pouring sugar in coffee.

Their food arrives, then they begin to eat. A male patron walk passes their table and eyes Yasmine lustfully. She giggles.

"Girl you get the men's attention even when sitting down. I thought it was that booty that drew them to you." Lenelle comments, chewing.

"I am just gorgeous from head to toe. Can't you see?" Yasmine jokes, biting into an eggroll.

Lenelle laughs, as she nods agreeing.

"SHE'S GAME"

After an hour has passed, Yasmine looks at her watch and realizes her lunch is over. The ladies pay for their meals, then exit the restaurant. Yasmine head to work and Lenelle head home to get some sleep before work.

On the way to the gym, Osai, exiting his office, spots Yasmine and approaches her.

"What do I have to do to get some of that?" He ask, eyeing her body, lustful.

"Fall asleep and dream about getting it. That's as close as you'll get to it." Yasmine replies sassy, then struts away.

"Wait, wait!" He yells and follows her.

"I got dollars with yo' face on 'em." Osai says, trying to speak cool.

Yasmine tells Osai that she heard he's frugal with his money and probably will not want to afford her high taste. She tells him the kind of car that is on her wish list. He offers to give her the down payment for it.

She thinks for a few seconds then hands him her business card.

"Call me when you're ready." She speaks, gamely.

"I will…and it will be our little secret." Osai says then proceed home.

A week later, Osai dials Yasmine and tells her he has the money and is ready for her. So, at lunch time, Yasmine dials Lenelle and ask does she want to hang out with her for lunch. Lenelle, just getting in from school, accepts the offer.

Yasmine says she'll pick up the food and be over in a few minutes.

Shortly afterwards, Yasmine arrives at Lenelle's condo building and dials her. When she answers, Yasmine hangs up in her face, then rushes to Osai's place. Lenelle dials her back and she doesn't answer.

"What the hell is up with her?" Lenelle ask.

Elsewhere, Yasmine and Osai are engaging in passionate sex. After thirty minutes, the intimacy ends. They take a brief shower and get dressed.

"Thanks for the down payment, even though I asked for more. Ten gs will make my note very reasonable, but I need the rest before I get the car." Yasmine says, demandingly.

"Thanks for that fat ass and don't worry about the rest...I'll get it to you! I want you to get kinky with me the next time." Osai says, putting on his doctor's coat.

"I only get that way with my hubby." Yasmine expresses, somewhat loyally.

"I'll make you loosen up." Osai comments, domineeringly.

Yasmine blows a kiss at Osai, then exits his place. As she approaches the elevator she dials Lenelle and when she answers, she ends the call. She gets on the crowded elevator then rushes out of the building to work.

When Yasmine enters the gym, her coworker Laila begin to sniff.

"You must have gone home and showered, because we do not use men's soap in the ladies' room." Laila comments.

"Yes, I did and accidentally used my husband's soap." Yasmine lies. "I had to go home and get me a quickie." Yasmine jokes, steady lying.

"It smells arousing." Laila compliments.

Yasmine smiles, then goes and work with her client.

"A FIBBING WHORE"

Later that night, Lenelle calls Yasmine and enquires about her hanging up in her face and not showing for lunch.

"Something came up at work. I tried to call you, but my battery went dead." Yasmine lies, ironing Deja's school clothes.

"I called you several times then ate a sandwich and went to sleep. Maybe we can meet tomorrow." Lenelle proposes.

"We will." Yasmine replies, then ends the call.

Lenelle puts on her uniform then heads to work.

The next morning, Yasmine is placing breakfast on the kitchen table for her family. She takes a seat and begin to eat.

"Mama I want some tennis shoes. I'm tired of wearing dressy shoes…I can't have playtime with the kids." Deja complains.

"You do not need to be running around like a wild animal. So, no tennis for you. You are a beautiful princess and you must look that way at all times." Yasmine replies, carelessly.

"That's boring." Deja mutters then continue eating.

After the family is done eating, Deja goes to the restroom and washes her hands. Yasmine cleans the table. While she's doing so, Ramone kisses the back of her neck and discovers a passion mark on her upper back.

"What's this?" He asks.

"I bruised myself when I fell down instructing one of my students." Yasmine fibs.

"I can't have all of this beauty with bruises on it. Are you ready to be a housewife?" Ramone ask, wishful.

"No, I love working." Yasmine replies.

"Well, be careful doing it." Ramone commands.

Deja returns to the kitchen with book bag in hand. Everyone kisses each other goodbye, then Yasmine and Deja exit the house to school. Ramone decides to work from home for the day.

Before doing so, he goes to the laundry room and sorts the dirty clothing to wash. He comes across Yasmine's workout gear that has a masculine aroma. He goes to the restroom and sniffs his soap and realizes it doesn't smell the same.

He dials Yasmine and confronts her about the smell. She replies that the ladies' room ran out of soap and used the soap from the men's locker room.

"Thank God! For a minute, I thought you were fooling around." Ramone says, relieved.

"Baby calm down. You know I am all into you. No one can take your place." Yasmine says, cunning, pulling up to Deja's school.

"Ok baby, I am gonna get busy. See you later." Ramone says, putting clothes in washing machine.

"Honey please pick up some Chinese food tonight. I am not in a cooking mood." Yasmine states.

Ramone complains that he doesn't want Chinese and agrees to cook dinner. Yasmine expresses her gratitude and love to him, then ends the call.

"A STRUMPET TRAINS"

Next, Deja exits the car to school, then Yasmine proceeds to work. After several hours of working, Yasmine calls Lenelle to join her for lunch and they meet up at a soul food restaurant. They converse over their meal.

"I'll be picking up that Carrera, soon." Yasmine brags, biting into a slice of hot water cornbread.

"So, you've decided to spend yo' dollars!" Lenelle says surprised.

"Yeah... I am blessed and need to stop being so cheap." Yasmine says insincerely.

"Am I dreaming?" Lenelle ask, pinching herself in disbelief.

Yasmine laughs.

"I wish I could live like you. Have a handsome man that loves and shares his wealth with me. And live in a luxurious mansion, instead of a one-bedroom apartment." Lenelle speaks, covetous. "But, I am thankful for what I have." Lenelle says, with a mouthful of collard greens. "I do feel I'll have the life I want someday."

"You will have to be patient and learn how to work your "ASS"ets." Yasmine advises. "Show them off more. Wear leggings and stilettos. Also, mini-dresses are a major plus. Trust me! You'll have so many men offering you money...you'll be dumping "Doc" in a heartbeat." Yasmine schools.

Lenelle nods agreeing, nibbling on a piece of chicken.

    One month later, Yasmine and Ramone give a 9-year wedding anniversary party at their home. Lenelle and Osai attend. Everyone's having a great time eating and chatting.

Lenelle's sporting multicolored paisley leggings, 3-inch stilettos and a black fitted blouse that props up her breast. Yasmine and Osai cover up their affair, very well.

"We are out of vodka!" One of the drunk guest yells.

"There's more in the kitchen. I'll get it." Ramone says then proceed to the kitchen.

"Bring the cake knife, baby!" Yasmine yells to Ramone.

Ramone enters the kitchen, grabs the items then return to the party. He and Yasmine then stand dressed in their wedding attire, before their pastor and the crowd of guest and renew their wedding vows.

"I Ramone and Yasmine Hampton do solemnly swear to love, honor and obey each other. We will not allow temptation or greed to destroy what God has joined together." The couple recites in unison.

Everyone applauses and cheers for them. The couple then serves everyone cake. Lenelle can barely eat her slice because she's busy crying uncontrollably as Osai eyes her with great concern.

"Girl quit clowning. You are embarrassing me." Osai complains, handing Lenelle a tissue.

"I want what Yasmine has." Lenelle replies, covetous, wiping her eyes.

Everyone laughs at her. Then, one of the female guest yells that she admires Yasmine's relationship as well, then begin to cry. Ramone shouts that the ceremony is supposed to be a joyous occasion.

"Everybody! Stop crying and dance!" Ramone yells.

The deejay then plays Lil' Wayne's "Earthquake", then the guest put their cake down and start grooving.

"NO FREE RIDE"

After the party ends, the guest hug and congratulate the couple on their way out. Osai and Lenelle enter the car then take off to home.

"Aren't they blessed? I wish I had a man that will share his success with me." Lenelle hints to Osai.

"I wish I had a woman to share her ass with me." Osai replies, belligerently.

"If you would show me that you are worthy of it, then I'll give it to you." Lenelle replies, angrily. "How can you own several businesses and not give me money?" Lenelle ask.

"Nothing is free in this world." He answers.

"Well on that note, I'll stop cooking, cleaning and massaging you for free. As of today, I'm charging. Why do you want me, if I am not putting out?" Lenelle inquires.

"You do cook a fire ass meatloaf." He replies idiotically.

"Well no more!" Lenelle yells.

"Ok, I will pay you one hundred dollars a month, but you got to throw some head in there." Osai insults.

"Stop the car! Stop it now!" She shouts.

Osai stops the car then Lenelle exits and slams the door shut. She grabs her cell phone from her purse and dials a cab.

"Girl get in…it's dangerous out there." Osai commands, caringly.

"Like you care about my safety. I am done with you…now go!" Lenelle hollers, pointing her finger up the highway.

"That's fine! I got plenty of "kitty" applications on file." Osai boast then take off speeding, leaving a trail of tire smoke in Lenelle's face.

Fifteen minutes later, the cab arrives. Lenelle enters crying uncontrollably. She gives the cabbie her address, then he take off to her home.

"Are you ok?" The cabbie ask with great concern. "Why are you out in the middle of nowhere looking so beautiful?" He probes.

"It's a horror story that I feel will have a happy ending." Lenelle replies, optimistically.

"I like your positive attitude. Not too many street women have one of those." He insinuates.

"I am not a whore! I just broke up with my boyfriend." She replies, offended.

The cabbie apologizes. After twenty minutes of driving, they arrive at her home. Lenelle hands the cabbie some cash, and he refuses to accept it.

"It's on me. I've had a prosperous day, so I am sharing my blessing with you. So, gorgeous lady, have a good night." The cabbie sympathizes.

"Thank you. It's been a while since a man has given me something." Lenelle comments.

"Oh, I can give you more than just free rides." The cabbie offers, handing Lenelle his business card.

She accepts it, then writes her number on the back of it and hands it to the cabbie. She then wishes him a safe night, while exiting the cab. She goes to her car.

"I'll be watching you!" He yells, interested.

Lenelle waves her hand goodbye to the cabbie then goes into her car and grabs her books, so she can study. The cabbie takes off after she enters the building.

Lenelle enters her apartment, kicks off her shoes, then goes to her bedroom and drops on the bed, exhaustingly. She lies staring at the ceiling.

"Why I can't meet a man better than Osai?" She talks to herself. "I don't want a damn cab driver." She complains.

She gets up and goes to the restroom and runs bath water.

"But then again, maybe a man with less money will treat me better." She mutters, removing her clothes.

She grabs a bottle of strawberry and cream bubble bath, then pours it into the water. She steps one foot into the tub, then remembers she wants to sip on an alcoholic beverage while soaking, for more relaxation. So, she exits the restroom butt naked to the kitchen and makes a fruity cocktail, loaded with rum.

While she is en route to the restroom, her phone rings. She answers, and it is the cabbie. Lenelle explains to him she is busy, and they will have to talk later.

He begs for Lenelle to give him a few minutes of conversation. She refuses, then ends the call.

"Yuck! He is so gross. But I might give him a chance." She utters to herself as she proceeds to the bathroom, sipping on beverage.

"CAN'T JUDGE A WHORE"

A week later, Yasmine gets off work still sporting her workout attire and goes to a jewelry store down the street from the gym, to get her wedding ring cleansed. Judge Jake Meyers enters the store and stares lustful at Yasmine's large butt, as she browses the collection of platinum diamond rings.

"Hello Mr. Meyers." The clerk greets, cheerfully.

He waves his hand at the clerk.

Yasmine picks out a ring of interest and tries it on. It's too large, so she asks for a smaller size and it fits perfectly.

"What's the cost?" She asks the store clerk.

"Ninety-five hundred." She answers.

Yasmine is not impressed with the price, so she takes the ring off and returns it to the clerk.

Jake approaches Yasmine.

"How are you?" He ask.

"Hello Jake…I'm fine." Yasmine replies.

"You said that right…you are most definitely, a fine woman." He compliments, eyeing her body desirously.

The clerk places the ring back into the case. Jake tells her to give the ring back to Yasmine. He pulls Yasmine to the side then they begin to whisper to each other.

"If you thank me later, I'll buy it for you." He offers.

Yasmine tells Jake that she'll have to refuse the offer, fearing Ramone will get suspicious. Because he knows how she spends her money on certain things.

"Tell him you've decided to spend your money on whatever you want, because that's what it is for." Jake concocts.

"How will I have to thank you?" Yasmine ask.

He looks at her private area.

"I will follow you to a hotel of your choice after we leave here. I need your number to text the room number to you. We don't need to be seen going in together." He plans, eagerly.

Yasmine gazes at the ring then agrees and gives him her business card. He pulls out his credit card and purchases the ring, then drops off his watch for repair.

Yasmine's wedding ring is finished being cleansed. So, she pays for the service, then puts it on.

Afterwards, Jake and Yasmine exits the store to their vehicles then take off to the hotel. They arrive at a ritzy downtown spot. He goes to the checkout counter and pays for a room.

He gets the key and goes to the room then text Yasmine the room number. She sneaks into the rear of the hotel to his room. When she enters, he's already nude and begin to quickly take off her clothes.

He begins to penetrate her vaginally and anally with his tongue. She enjoys it so much, she doesn't make him use a condom during intercourse. An hour later, the sexual encounter is over, so Yasmine rushes to the restroom and showers, then gets dressed.

"I enjoyed you. We have got to do it again." Jake suggest, lying in the bed smoking a cigarette.

"No, I can't jeopardize my marriage or career. Remember, I work with your wife." Yasmine rejects, assertively.

"My soon-to-be ex-wife. But, I understand. You were worth the cost. Call me if you have a change of mind." He offers.

She blows him a kiss, then grabs her purse and exits the room.

"A SECRET ADMIRER"

Twenty minutes later, Yasmine arrives home and enters. She kisses her family, then goes into the kitchen to cook.

"Baby thanks for taking the pork chops out of the freezer!" She yells.

"Deja did it!" Ramone responds.

"Well thanks for teaching her!" Yasmine hollers, taking vegetables from the refrigerator.

"No problem…that's what daddy is for!" He shouts, jokey.

Deja enters the kitchen and offers to help with dinner. Yasmine assigns her to cut up the onion for the stew.

"Yuck…that's smelly." Deja replies, grabbing a knife and cutting board.

After an hour has passed, they are done cooking and now eating their meal. Yasmine flashes her ring in Ramone's face.

"Did you steal my credit card?" Ramone ask, buttering his bread.

"No, honey. I've decided to spend my money more often. If you don't use a blessing, you will lose it." Yasmine pretends.

"Well keep up the good work." Ramone replies, joyful.

"Baby I can't take you for granted. I love you too much." Yasmine says cunningly, as she slices her chops.

Later, dinner is over and Deja's helping Yasmine with the dishes and Ramone is gone to the store for cigarettes. The phone rings and Yasmine answers.

"What's up sis?" Lenelle ask.

"You are!" Yasmine answers, jokingly.

"I'm calling to let you know that I dumped Osai and he didn't care at all." Lenelle says, forlorn.

She informs Yasmine that his cheapness led to the breakup. Yasmine advises her to work what her mother gave her. Lenelle says she wants to take a break from dating and focus on her education, instead.

"Go ahead and be a nun…that sounds exciting." Yasmine says, sarcastic, washing a plate.

"At least I'll spare some tears." Lenelle says, guardedly.

"You got a good point." Yasmine agrees.

Lenelle tells Yasmine that she's heading to the community center to exercise, before she goes to work. They plan to chat tomorrow then end the call.

Twenty minutes later, Lenelle arrives at the center and swims a few laps. Afterwards, she showers, gets dressed then exits the center to her car. As she approaches it, she finds a greeting card on the windshield.

She removes and reviews its reading: **"It's not what's on the outside, but what's on the inside that makes a woman beautiful."** She smiles and looks around for a suspicious person and sees no one then enters her car. She take off in transit to home to get ready for work.

As Lenelle commutes, she grins with enjoyment at the fact that someone desires and sees her worth.

"FLEA POWDER, PLEASE!"

A few days later, Yasmine's at work exercising with a client when suddenly her vagina begins to itch badly. The irritation is so intense, it makes her itch all over. She rushes to the restroom, then runs into a bathroom stall and removes her clothing.

She then deeply scratches her vagina. Afterwards, she inspects her workout gear for mites.

"Are you ok?" Her coworker, Kenise Meyers, ask.

"Yes, I just need to start changing my clothes after I work out! I think I have a yeast infection…I am itching like crazy!" Yasmine shares, holding her vagina.

"I shower and change clothes every day after work and haven't gotten an infection, yet." Kenise responds, drying her hands.

      Yasmine sits on the toilet and urinate, then experiences severe burning. She places her hand over her mouth to hold in her scream. She then puts on her clothes and exits the stall.

Yasmine takes off her rings and washes her hands. Kenise notices her new ring and compliments it, then exits the restroom to the work floor. Yasmine, still experiencing vaginal discomfort, dries her hands, then exits the restroom and approach Kenise.

She tells her she has an emergency, so she needs to leave. Kenise, a fitness instructor, take on Yasmine's client. Yasmine grabs her belongings, then rushes out of the gym to her car, an hour before her lunch.

As she unlocks the car door, Osai, on his way home, passes the gym. He spots Yasmine then pulls up beside her.

"I need you, now!" He says, eagerly.

"Not now. I'm in a hurry." She replies, nervously.

"I don't expect a response like that after dropping off a five-figure check! But, I'll go ahead and give you the rest." Osai offers, desperately.

"I'm on the way." Yasmine replies, without demur.

Yasmine trails Osai to his condo building.

She hides her vehicle around the corner, not wanting Lenelle to see it. He exits his car to his place. Yasmine dials Lenelle and ask her to join her for lunch at a new restaurant that's ten minutes away.

"You are going to lunch a little early." Lenelle comments.

"I didn't eat breakfast, so I am starving." Yasmine fibs.

"Ok, I'll go." Lenelle says.

"I am leaving now to pick you up." Yasmine says, exiting her car.

She ends the call and rushes into the building to Osai's place. When she enters, he begins to passionately kiss her. He walks her to the bedroom and lies her on the bed. They then begin to take off each other's clothes.

He opens her legs and attempt to perform oral sex on her. Yasmine pushes him away because of her vaginal condition, then performs oral sex on him. After she finishes, Osai attempts to have unprotected sex with her.

She stops him then removes a condom from her purse and makes him put it on. She then engages in painful intercourse. She lies tearful and frightened, thinking it's something worse than a yeast infection.

The encounter ends then Yasmine quickly wipes her teary eyes and rushes to the restroom. She cleanses herself with baby wipes. Afterwards, she exits the restroom and hastily grabs her purse, then attempts to exit the bedroom.

"I can't get enough of you." Osai says, pulling Yasmine to him. "I want to stop using condoms and get real nasty with you…please loosen up!" He begs.

Elsewhere, Lenelle is impatiently pacing the floor, awaiting Yasmine's arrival.

"Where is that girl? It's been forty minutes…she's only five minutes away." Lenelle rants, looking out of her 10 story window with binoculars.

She dials Yasmine for the 3rd time and gets no response. So, she goes into the kitchen and prepares lunch, assuming she's not coming.

      At Osai's place, Yasmine's sitting on his lap. She's enquiring about keeping up their affair while Lenelle is living in the same building. She fears they'll eventually be exposed.

"I'll find a way to get her evicted." He responds, cruelly.

"No. That's a little too dirty. You must remember she's my family and I love her. Plus, she loves living here." Yasmine expresses, caringly.

"I apologize." Osai says, phony.

"I'll move when my lease is up, next year." Osai says.

Yasmine begins to have vaginal itching and burning, so she hops off of Osai's lap.

"I really have to attend my daughter's play." Yasmine lies, rushing out of the room.

"Call me tomorrow!" Osai yells, as Yasmine exits his place.

As she rushes to the elevator her vaginal discomfort worsens to the point she can't tolerate it. So, she goes into the garbage chute and severely scratches her vagina, then puts hand lotion on it to soothe the burning.

"I have never experienced such pain. Giving birth felt better than whatever this is." She murmurs to herself.

An elderly man exiting the elevator hears Yasmine's rant, then opens the garbage chute door.

"Honey who are you talking to?" He ask, Yasmine.

"Oh sir, I was on the phone. I just ended the call. Excuse me." She says, exiting to the elevator.

"THAT GIRL IS ON FIRE"

Before she enters, she dials Lenelle and when she answers, Yasmine hangs up in her face. She then gets on the elevator and rushes out of the building.

Yasmine gets in her vehicle and goes to the doctor's office and learns that she has a curable STD.

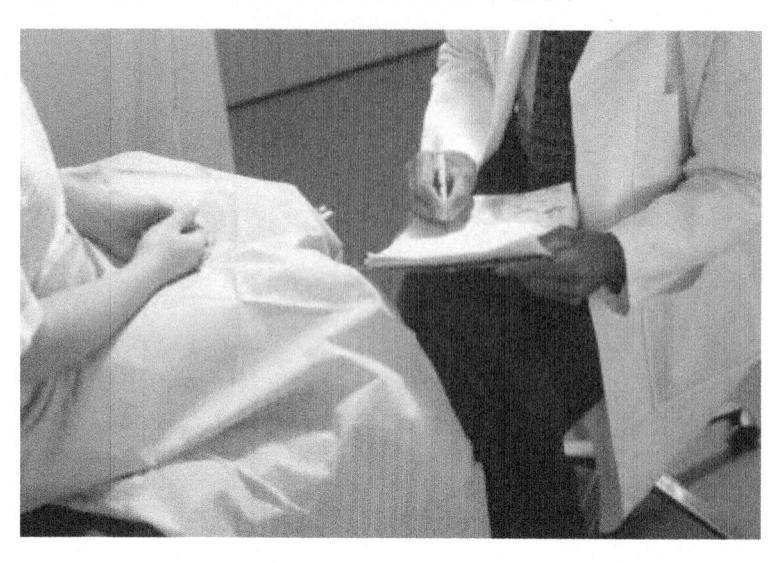

The doctor instructs her to not have sex for a week, until it cures. Yasmine is furious and storms out of the office to her car.

She doesn't know whether Jake or Ramone infected her. She decides to keep it a secret, until one of them mentions it. She then proceed to the pharmacy and gets her prescription.

Afterwards, she take off in transit to her home, then her cell phone rings and she answers.

"Why did you not show?" Lenelle ask, irately.

"One of my clients popped up at the last minute. I tried to call and cancel with you, but my phone dropped the call. I am sorry." Yasmine tells an untruth.

"No problem and goodbye." Lenelle says, slightly suspicious, then ends the call.

A couple of nights later, Lenelle is on the way to work when she receives a call from Osai.

"What do you want?!" She ask, furiously.

"You need to come by and pick up yo' belongings and leave my door key...ASAP!" Osai commands, rudely.

"No problem! I will be there in the morning when I get off of work." She responds, sassy.

"Try to get here before I go to work." Osai says, demandingly.

Lenelle informs him that she sometimes works overtime which will cause her to miss him. Osai rudely refers to Lenelle's belongings as "junk" and tells her that it will be in the study next to the trash can. Lenelle ends the call.

"I hate that asshole!" She yells, banging on the steering wheel.

Later, she arrives at work and enters looking sadly.

"Smile! You got a job...be happy!" Her coworker, Felix, kids. "What's wrong?" He ask.

"It's a man thing." She mutters.

"Something the majority of women have." Felix comments.

Lenelle giggles then clocks in and proceed to her desk for work.

The next morning at the end of her shift, she's told she has to work overtime. After doing so, she clocks out then exits the workplace to her car. She proceeds to Osai's home.

When she arrives, he's already left. So, she goes into the study and grabs her stuff. She then opens his desk drawer and puts in the door key and finds a copy of the check Osai gave to Yasmine.

"Why the fuck did he give my sister a check and give me nothing?" She questions angrily.

She thinks for a second.

"That whore been screwing my man!" She yells. "That slut!"

She grabs her cell phone to call and confront Yasmine, then pauses.

"No! I am a peacemaker, so I will keep my silence. God will get her for me." She vents to herself, placing her phone in the purse.

She takes a seat and cries.

"That bitch was calling my house phone and setting up fake lunch gatherings, because she wanted to make sure I was in my apartment and not catch her coming to and from Osai's place!" Lenelle berates.

"A LOT OF FREAKING GOING ON"

Lenelle stands and paces the floor, crying uncontrollably. She then pulls herself together and exits Osai's place to school. While in class, she cannot focus because of the thought of Yasmine and Osai's affair, so she rushes out of the class to the restroom.

"Lord help me keep my peaceful nature and do not allow me to be vengeful." She mutters.

Lenelle exits the school to her vehicle and take off to home. She passes a gun shop on the way, then does a U-turn and enter the store. She shops for a gun to shoot Yasmine and Osai then pauses.

"Don't do it! You have a bright future ahead of you!" An auditory hallucination tells her.

Lenelle puts down the gun, then rushes out of the store to her vehicle. She dials her mother, Clara.

"Hi my darling baby!" Clara answers, jovially.

"Mom I need to talk." Lenelle says, hurtful.

"What is it?" She ask.

"Yasmine has been sleeping with Osai. I am so devastated, I want to drop out of school. I am thinking of popping pills to ease the pain." Lenelle cries.

    Clara tells Lenelle to not let someone else's wrongdoing stop her from being successful. She advises her to pray for strength to deal with the hurt, instead of taking drugs and to continue her education. Lenelle cheers up and thanks Clara for the pep talk, then ends the call.

Later that night, Yasmine has just finished helping Deja with her homework. She tucks her into bed then exits to her bedroom.

"Get out of this damn bed!" She yells to the family dog, Mystro.

He runs out of the room. Ramone is in bed working on his laptop.

"Come here sexy and give me some of that sweet stuff." Ramone says seductive, pulling Yasmine's arm.

"Let me get a bath first." Yasmine says, not wanting to have sex because of the disease.

"I'll take you funky." He says, greatly lusting for her.

She smiles and heads to the bathroom and he follows. They take a hot, steamy and romantic shower together then exits the bathroom soaking wet, to the bedroom. Ramone lies Yasmine on the bed and kisses her breast and stomach, then attempts to perform oral sex on her.

Fearing he will catch the STD in his mouth, Yasmine pushes his head away then performs oral sex on him. Afterwards, Ramone attempts to perform orally again.

"Stop!" Yasmine says firmly, pushing his head away.

"What's the problem? You usually love for me to do that." Ramone probes, suspiciously.

"I have a yeast infection from my dirty workout clothes. So, no carpet munching for a week." Yasmine orders.

He gets on top of her to engage in intercourse then Yasmine stops him.

"Get a condom." She commands.

"We haven't used those since you got the damn NuvaRing!" Ramone fusses, irritably.

"The yeast might bite you." Yasmine jokes.

Ramone giggles, grabs a condom from the nightstand drawer and puts it on. They then engage in intercourse for the next hour.

Elsewhere, Kenise is at Jake's place getting her belongings when she finds a receipt for a women's diamond ring. She goes to the computer and googles the items barcode number, to see how the ring looks. Then, an image of a ring identical to Yasmine's, appears.

She gets furious and dials Jake. He answers.

"Are you fucking Yasmine?!" She yells.

"We are divorcing each other, so I can do what I damn well please!" Jake yells, combatively.

"But, we are still having sex with each other. I am glad I made yo' ass use protection!" Kenise hollers, then ends the call.

Kenise plans to play it cool with Yasmine to keep her job, until her divorce is final. Then, she will receive alimony payments.

A week later, Lenelle is exiting her condo building in workout attire. She's going for a jog, when the cabbie drives pass her place. He spots her then pauses the cab.

"Are you gonna let me spoil you tonight?" He ask Lenelle.

"I will let you know." She yells, then continues jogging.

The cabbie drives off.

Later that night, Lenelle exits her condo dressed alluringly, then enters her car. She meets up with her date at a ritzy restaurant for dinner.

After dining, they go to her place and have passionate sex.

The next morning, Lenelle awakens in a sullen mood, due to guilt of fornicating. She drags about slowly as she cooks breakfast. Her phone rings, then she answers.

It's her date, thanking her for such a wonderful time.

"You're welcomed. I also had fun." Lenelle replies, with a dull tone.

"You don't sound like you had a good time." Her date replies.

"I am just tired. Let me call you after I am done eating." Lenelle says, flipping omelet.

She then ends the call. Lenelle begin to eat.

Afterwards, she gets dressed for church. When she arrives, she realizes she's picked the perfect Sunday to attend. Because the pastor is sermonizing about "Forgiveness", which she is having difficulty giving to Yasmine.

After a couple of hours of service, Lenelle exits the church feeling holy.

"LITTLE SIS CATERS"

A week later, Yasmine is at the workplace engaging in a grueling workout session with a client. Around noon she clocks out for lunch. She goes into the locker room to get her coin purse and finds Kenise, sobbing.

"What's wrong?" Yasmine asks.

"This divorce is taking a toll on me. I feel I need some "psych pills" to cope! These brownies help relieve some of the pain." Kenise vents, shamelessly. "Want one?" She offers Yasmine, taking a bite of the treat.

"I don't need them." Yasmine replies, pointing at her butt. "But, if you need psychiatric help, then it is not a bad thing… it's a smart thing! I'd rather you see a professional, instead of self-medicating with illegal drugs." Yasmine encourages.

Kenise talks Yasmine into trying the treat and deviously eyes her as she joyfully chews it. Yasmine gives

Kenise a hug and tells her to pray about her situation, then exits the room.

Yasmine exits the gym and dials Lenelle, that's at home cooking. She wipes her hands on her apron then answers the phone. It's Yasmine offering for them to hook up for lunch.

Even though Lenelle is still having a little difficulty forgiving Yasmine. She accepts the offer.

Lenelle informs her that she's won a $500 grocery gift card and that she is cooking lunch for now on, instead of going out to eat.

"What are you making?" Yasmine asks.

"Taco salad and soft-shell chicken tacos." Lenelle replies, heating the vegetables.

"Wow, I am on the way." Yasmine states excitedly, then ends the call.

Yasmine arrives and begin to eat with Lenelle.

"This taco salad is great. And who taught you how to cook like this?" Yasmine praises.

"I taught myself...I didn't learn everything from you." Lenelle responds, biting a taco.

"And that's why you are broke." Yasmine criticizes.

"I feel I won't be for long. I've picked up a little game from you." Lenelle hints.

Yasmine goes into the kitchen and gets a glass of lemonade.

"You should have learned something after being my stepsister for seven years." Yasmine says.

"It's just not showing yet. But, it will in due time." Lenelle promises, pouring taco sauce on salad.

Yasmine ask Lenelle has she found out who's been placing the notes on her car. Yasmine believes it is the cabbie, that's stalking Lenelle. She states that she called him.

"What was he talking about?" Yasmine inquires, anxiously.

"Good stuff...very good stuff!" Lenelle responds, happily.

"Be sure you show off those gorgeous legs and prop up the tatas." Yasmine schools, drinking lemonade.

"I already have." Lenelle says, naughtily.

Yasmine begins to feel woozy. The last time she felt this way she was having a relapse of anxiety and depression from her mother's death.

"I still have nightmares...the antidepressants did not cure me." Yasmine open up.

"You might be relapsing like you did a year and a half ago and didn't know it...and landed in the hospital." Lenelle says, concerned.

Yasmine exits the kitchen to the living room couch and lies down.

Lenelle's father and Yasmine's mother were married and killed in a car accident. Lenelle handled her father's death well, because they were not close.

"I wanted to kill the driver that took my mother. I loved her so much." Yasmine cries, massaging her forehead.

"I feel you. My mom and I have a wonderful relationship...I wish she didn't live a thousand miles away." Lenelle comments, giving Yasmine a glass of water.

A week later, Yasmine wakes up groggy. She staggers into the living room and sees Ramone with a women's necklace.

"Thank you, baby." She says, reaching for the necklace.

"This isn't for you. It's a signing bonus for my new artist." Ramone says, placing it in a gift box.

"Are you sure?" Yasmine ask, distrusting.

"What's yo' problem? I've bought female artists gifts before. So, why are you screening me after five years of doing so?" Ramone questions, curiously.

Yasmine shakes her head confused, then pours a cup of coffee. Ramone tells Yasmine that she's acting like she's relapsing. She disagrees and claims she feels overworked.

Ramone kisses Yasmine then grabs his briefcase and exits the house to work. Yasmine turns on the TV to the soap operas and drinks her coffee. She forgot to discuss an issue with Ramone, so she dials him.

"What's up baby?" Ramone answers.

"I am going to get the Porsche today. Will you go with me?" She ask.

"Since you are buying it brand new, you don't need me to check it out...it's under warranty. Plus, it's a busy day for me." He responds, cranking the car.

"I don't understand why you are working on a Saturday." Yasmine says suspiciously.

Ramone claims he's worked on the weekend several times and that she needs to see her doctor for paranoia. Yasmine becomes irate and ends the call. Deja comes downstairs to the living room and ask Yasmine to cook her some chocolate chip pancakes.

Yasmine refuses and tells Deja to prepare a bowl of cereal.

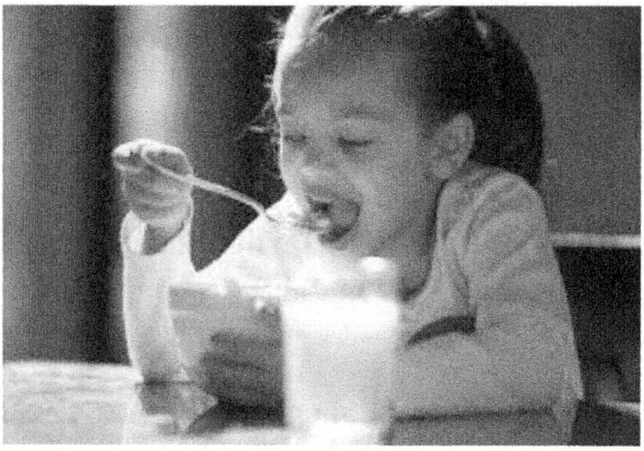

"SOMEBODY'S WATCHING"

Two weeks later, Yasmine enters the gym's locker room and overhears Kenise arguing on the phone with Jake. When she notices her presence, she ends the call.

"Girl that man is giving me the blues." Kenise complains.

"How is he, if you all are living separately?" Yasmine pries.

"He contracted a disease about a month ago and is blaming me, but I am fine! I'm a fool for screwing him, anyway. It's his adulterous ways that led to us divorcing!" Kenise vents, shamelessly.

Yasmine smiles with relief knowing that the STD didn't come from Ramone. She advises Kenise to be strong, then exits to the work floor.

"You bitch!" Kenise mumbles to herself, badmouthing Yasmine.

Later, Yasmine clocks out for lunch then her phone rings. She answers and it is Osai. He offers her $2000 to hook up with him and she accepts.

Yasmine then walks to Osai's condo building. Before she enters, she calls Lenelle and pretend that she's coming to her place for lunch. After their conversation, she rushes into the building to Osai's place.

Osai's neighbor, Rebecca, that has a crush on him, frowns at Yasmine as she knocks at his door. Osai opens it and she enters. He hands Yasmine the payment.

"Are you doing your neighbor?" Yasmine ask, placing the check in her coin purse.

"No. Why do you ask?" He replies, taking off his clothes.

"She mean mugged me!" She replies, getting undressed.

"Maybe she's my secret admirer!" Osai jokes.

They then have sex.

Afterwards, Osai prepares them coffee. While they are enjoying the beverage, he receives a text message from an unknown number reading: **"THAT MARRIED WOMAN WILL SEND YOU TO JAIL AND HELL!"** He fears he is being watched, so he rushes Yasmine out of his place.

Rebecca, coming from the store, exits the elevator as Yasmine approaches it.

"I see you sporting a wedding ring. Why are you going to Osai's?" She confronts, psychotically.

"You need to mind your own business," Yasmine replies, trying to get on the elevator.

Rebecca blocks Yasmine's entry to the elevator.

"What's your damn problem? Move!" Yasmine yells, irate.

"I've seen y'all kissing in the hall through my peephole...you slut!" Rebecca insults, placing her bag on the floor.

She then boldly slaps Yasmine's cheek.

"You are a psycho!" Yasmine hollers.

Yasmine, skilled in martial arts, makes a knock out move on her, then gets on the elevator.

The sexual encounter has left Yasmine hungry, so she decides to go to Lenelle's place.

"What took you so long?" Lenelle ask, irritated. "Your food is cold."

"One of my clients got injured and I had to write up an accident report." Yasmine fabricates.

"Are they ok?" Lenelle ask, putting Yasmine's food in the microwave.

"She will be." Yasmine replies.

Lenelle inquires about the bruise on Yasmine's cheek.

"My client accidentally hit me while doing jumping-jacks." She lies, nervously.

    Yasmine eats her lunch. After she's finished, she goes into the kitchen and places the dirty dishes in the sink. On the way out, she sees Lenelle's brand new Gucci handbag.

"Is this bootleg?" She ask, inspecting the bag.

"No, it's the real deal." Lenelle replies, prideful.

"You have never had this kind of taste or money. What are you doing?" Yasmine ask, nosey.

Lenelle looks guilty.

"You are doing Mr. Cabbie!" Yasmine accuses.

Lenelle laughs.

Yasmine is grateful for Lenelle finding a man to cater to her. But, is curious as to how a cab driver can afford such an expensive purse. Lenelle tells her he has a second job and no children.

"Did I tell you I got the Porsche?" Yasmine boast.

"Wow!" Lenelle replies, fascinated.

"Deja will be attending a slumber party soon, so I will be free to pick you up and drive you around then." Yasmine offers.

Next, Yasmine returns to work and begin to exercise. She suddenly gets dizzy.

"Are you ok?" Her client asks.

"I don't know." Yasmine replies, taking a seat.

The client goes to get help. Kenise arrives and pours cold water on Yasmine. She feels better.

"What caused that feeling?" Yasmine ask, then proceed to work out.

Later that night, Yasmine and her family are at the bowling alley. Rebecca gives her the evil-eye. Yasmine feels she is about to start trouble, so she goes to the restroom.

Rebecca follows her inside.

"What a lovely family you are fucking over. I wish I was that blessed. It is whores like you that make it difficult for us single women to find a good man!" Rebecca berates, boldly.

"You either zip it up or get zipped up! You have no man because you are fat and ugly!" Yasmine threatens and insults. "But, I can help your big, whale ass! Call me." She degrades, handing Rebecca her business card.

Rebecca stares at Yasmine, wrathfully, as she exits the restroom.

Yasmine and her family exits the venue and takeoff en route to home. Yasmine is very quiet throughout their journey, thinking of Rebecca's behavior.

"Are you ok baby? You are not talking." Ramone probes.

"I am just a little tired…that's all." She replies, innocent.

The next day, Rebecca leaves her apartment door opened as she takes the trash to the garbage chute. Osai just arriving home from the gym, smells a sweet aroma coming from her home.

"That smells great…what is it?" He ask, Rebecca.

"I am making red velvet cupcakes for my bakery. I'll give you one." She offers, seductive.

"Oh no, I am not a fan of sweets." He rejects.

She ignores him and gives him one of the treats and he tries and loves it.

"You should be a new client of mine and give the goods to that nice lady that comes to your place." Rebecca bargains, sneakily.

"Have a dozen of them ready for me soon." He replies, handing her cash.

"Thanks a lot." She replies, closing the door. "Now I can fix that cheating ass harlot." Rebecca rants to herself, grabbing a bottle of poison.

A few days later, Osai's order of cupcakes have arrived. He calls Yasmine on her lunch break.

"Hey baby, stop by for a minute. I got a treat for you." He invites.

Shortly afterwards, Yasmine calls Lenelle and makes plans to come over for lunch, then ends the call and rushes to

Osai's place. He gives her the bake goods and she tries one and loves it.

"How did you know red velvet is my favorite?" She ask Osai, impressed.

He grins.

She can't just eat one of the treats, so she consumes another one. Osai tries to have sex with her, but she can't due to her menstrual cycle. Yasmine grabs the goods and exits his place to Lenelle's.

"You can't stay long because I have to pick up my work uniform from the cleaners." Lenelle says, handing Yasmine a sub sandwich and soup that she prepared.

Yasmine hurriedly eats the meal, then returns to work. She begins to workout with her client, then gets dizzy and faints. Her client screams for help and one of the employees calls the ambulance.

They arrive and transport Yasmine to the hospital. When a toxicology report is done, Thorazine (an antipsychotic drug used as a sedative and tranquilizer), is found in her system. The nurse telephones Ramone and informs him of Yasmine's condition.

He quickly arrives at the hospital.

"What's the name of your wife's psychiatrist?" The doctor ask.

"I am not aware that she's seeing one. Why do you ask?" Ramone replies, confused.

"There are "psych meds" in her system." The doctor informs.

"What?!" Ramone ask in shock.

The doctor states that she's stable and will release her soon.

After an hour has passed, she's released from the hospital. On the way home, her and Ramone chat.

"Are you seeing a shrink?" Ramone questions.

"No Ramone, I am not and do not know where the meds came from." She denies, angrily.

"If you are still suffering from your mother's death you can talk to me." Ramone insinuates.

"I am fine darling. Something strange is going on. The only psychiatrist I know is Osai." Yasmine states.

Ramone feels Osai may have poisoned her at their anniversary party. Yasmine argues that it has been over a month since the party and the effect wouldn't take that long to show. Ramone agrees, leaving him confused.

Yasmine stares out of the window, having a flashback to when Osai stated that he will make her kinky in bed. She's thinking he has been poisoning her.

The couple pick up Deja from school. She enters shocked to see both her parents pick her up.

"Daddy you must have taken off today to take mama on a date." Deja states, smiling.

"Mama got sick and couldn't drive home. So I picked her up from work." Ramone replies.

"What's wrong with you mama?" She ask.

"I ate something bad." Yasmine lies.

Deja kisses her on the cheek and tells her to get well.

The family arrive home and Ramone heat up fish sticks and fries for dinner. Yasmine doesn't eat due to lack of appetite, but instead goes to bed.

"WHO'S CRAZY?"

A week later, Ramone drives Yasmine to work after she's been off to rest.

"I hope my car has not been stolen or vandalized." Yasmine says, eating a sausage biscuit.

"I'm sure it's fine…I was too busy to pick it up." Ramone replies.

They arrive at the gym then approach Yasmine's Porsche, inspects it and finds it in great condition. They kiss each other, then Yasmine enters the workplace. Ramone take off to work.

After a few hours of working, Yasmine takes a lunch break. She grabs a granola bar and apple juice from the snack machine then exits the gym to her car. She dials Osai.

"Hey baby." He answers, sitting on the couch watching TV. "Yasmine, we have got to take a break!" He says firmly, fearing he's being spied on.

"That's not why I am calling you. Have you been poisoning me with "crazy meds"?" She ask, nibbling on granola bar.

"Hell no! I will lose my license and go to jail for that!" He yells, offended.

"It seems like after I ate the cupcakes I got extremely ill. Where did you get them?" Yasmine ask, suspicious.

"From my neighbor Rebecca. She owns the "Sweetest Bakery" on Third Street." He replies.

"If I had known that, I would not have eaten them because she attacked me!" Yasmine yells, angrily.

Yasmine tells Osai that the meds were found in her system. He is shocked and expresses great concern for her health. She informs him that she's fine.

"Has Rebecca been in your home?" She ask, hysterical.

"Only once for some sugar." He replies.

"She probably stole the meds from your home and poisoned me. Damn!" Yasmine shouts.

"She did not go past my kitchen…she could not have poisoned you!" Osai responds, furious and ends the call.

He later slides a letter under Rebecca's door saying he is no longer patronizing her business, because of her feuding with Yasmine. He threatens to go to the police and sue her in court, if she doesn't provide them with a peaceful environment.

Rebecca picks up the letter and reviews it.

"I should have went ahead and poisoned that whore, like I planned to!" She shouts, ripping the letter.

She fears she will lose her freedom and business, so she leaves them alone.

A few days later, the weekend is here, so Yasmine and Lenelle are out cruising in the Porsche.

"I am gonna get one of these." Lenelle says confidently, patting on the dashboard.

    A couple weeks later, Kenise wants confirmation of Jake and Yasmine's affair, so she steals a picture of Yasmine from her purse, then exits the gym. She goes to the jewelry store and shows the photo to the clerk and ask has she seen her. The clerk, unaware of whom Kenise is, tells her that Yasmine was there with Jake and that he bought her a ring.

Kenise's jaw drops, then she runs furiously out of the store.

A week later, when Kenise gets to work, she gives Yasmine a dozen of homemade brownies. Yasmine eats one and puts the rest in her locker then goes to lunch.

    She dials Lenelle and offers a lunch date. She rejects, because she has to attend school and take her finals. Lenelle offers to fix Yasmine a plate of food that she cooked.

    Yasmine accepts the offer. On the way to Lenelle's place, Osai calls her and cries that he misses her. He offers her $1000 to hookup.

Yasmine agrees to come to his place. She first goes to Lenelle's and get the plate. She then rushes to the elevator, so Lenelle won't see her going to Osai's.

She arrives and Osai opens the door. Yasmine enters.

"Mmmm, that smells good." Osai says.

"Lenelle made it." Yasmine responds, uncovering the meal.

"I won't be eating that." He says, distrusting.

Yasmine ask Osai for a glass of water. He goes into the kitchen and gets it.

When Yasmine's done eating her meal, Osai pays her for sex. After they finish intercourse, she takes a wash up then exits his place. She then dials Lenelle to learn of her whereabouts, so she won't catch her exiting the building.

"Girl are you still at home?" She ask, sneakily.

"No...on my way to school. I am so glad it's my last day!" Lenelle replies.

"I am calling to let you know that the meal was damn good." Yasmine fakes.

"Thank you and I will speak with you later." Lenelle replies, weary of Yasmine's games.

Yasmine rushes out of the building en route to work. On the way, she staggers and falls. A couple of bystanders come to her aid.

"Do you need someone to transport you to your destination?" A female bystander ask, helping Yasmine to her feet.

"I feel I can make. I am just a little dizzy." She replies, holding her head, staggering.

"Here! Drink this water. Maybe you are dehydrated." The male bystander offers, handing Yasmine bottled water.

She drinks it and begin to feel much better.

"FINALLY! A COMMITTED WHORE"

Yasmine returns to work and begin to exercise then she faints. Kenise rushes to her and pours a bottle of water onto her face. Yasmine awakens.

"You need a pregnancy test." Kenise suggest.

"I've had one and there is no bread in this oven." Yasmine speaks, drowsily.

"Do you want me to call the ambulance?" Kenise ask, pretending to care.

"No. I feel I can drive myself." Yasmine replies, struggling to get off the floor. "I am gonna take a leave of absence until I can find out what's wrong with me."

Yasmine grabs her belongings, then staggers out of the gym to her car. She takes off in transit to home. She's veering in and out of traffic.

A cop notices her inappropriate driving, so he follows her. The blaring of the police car's siren alerts Yasmine of the cop's trailing, so she pulls over.

"Miss, get out of the car!" The cop orders.

"I can't." Yasmine says slurred, with her tongue protruding.

She's very sweaty and dazed looking.

"Can you tell me your name?" The cop evaluates.

"Stop trying to hit on me…I don't do cops." Yasmine responds, incoherently.

The cop realizes she's not stable, so he turns off her car and removes the keys. He then dials the ambulance. They arrive to the scene shortly afterwards, then take Yasmine to the hospital.

"She's back!" The doctor says, surprised.

The nurse draws her blood and do another toxicology report and finds the same antipsychotic drug is in her system. The paramedics transport Yasmine to a psychiatric facility, obeying the doctor's order. The staff calls Ramone and informs him that they need him at St. Lucas Mental Hospital.

He later arrives and signs the admission papers then exits the hospital to work. He enters his office and takes a seat at his desk. He dials Lenelle and explains Yasmine's situation and ask can Deja stay with her during the day, since college is out for the summer.

Lenelle agrees.

Then, a sultry young female singing artist, dressed very enticingly, enters his office. She walks with effortless grace to Ramone and eyes him suggestively, as she places her CD on his desk.

"Lenelle, let me call you later." Ramone says, eyeing the woman desirously. He then ends the call.

The young lady then walks away and exits the office. Ramone then receives a text message of Yasmine and Osai having sex. He watches in anger, then slams the phone on the desk.

"My money is going to a woman that needs and deserves it." Ramone says, staring at the young lady's CD.

"A COURTESAN OUT OF BUSINESS"

A month later, Kenise goes to the hospital and visits a stable and alert Yasmine. She has a slight mouth twitch, as a side effect from the medicines. Yasmine doesn't seem to be enthusiastic about her presence.

"Did you poison those brownies with meds?" Yasmine ask, with a speech impairment.

"Why would I do that?" Kenise ask, innocently.

"Because Jake told me you asked if we have been screwing each other." Yasmine replies, hostile.

"I am not into poisoning my enemy, but I will bake my shit into their brownies!" Kenise responds, impishly. "Here's a toothbrush!" Kenise mocks, placing the grooming tool on the bed.

Yasmine yells for her to leave. Kenise rushes out of the room, laughing.

Lenelle then enters the room. Yasmine's glad to see her.

"I love your Jimmy Choo shoes. You have really stepped yo' game up." Yasmine compliments. "Did Mr. Cabbie buy them?" She ask.

"I guess you can say he did. I've been receiving a monthly allowance from him." Lenelle brags.

"Wait a minute! That necklace looks like Ramone's artist's gift." Yasmine says.

She then thinks to herself.

"I'm sorry, these meds they are forcing in me, got me hallucinating." She says, thinking she's unbalanced.

"No, they don't! This necklace was never for his artist, but for me. Ramone is now giving me your three gs a month." Lenelle reveals, boldly. "That's how I got the Gucci and everything else. Soon I'll have your Porsche." She promises, cold-heartedly.

"What the fuck are you doing talking crazy to me?" Yasmine ask, rowdily. "Do you need the damn "happy pills"?" Yasmine insults.

Lenelle laughs.

Yasmine yells that Lenelle will never be her and that she looks ten times better and always has. Lenelle belligerently claims to already be her. She informs Yasmine that Ramone has filed for divorce because she provided him with video proof of her affair with Osai.

"I am now living in your home, fucking your man that has paid off my student loans and caring for your child." Lenelle exposes, boldly. "My wish has come true…thanks to your advice! Ramone loved me in those leggings and stilettos that I wore to you all's anniversary party. So much, he started putting notes and cards on my car." Lenelle mocks.

Yasmine yells for her to get out. Lenelle tells her she didn't want to hurt her by seeing her man. But, when she found out she was being a scandalous whore with her boyfriend, she decided to use the harlot skills Yasmine taught her, against her.

"When I found that copy of the check he wrote to you I couldn't forget or forgive you all…no matter how much I prayed and went to church. Lord, please forgive me for this one. But, sometimes your vengeance takes too long." Lenelle gabs.

"When I get out of here…I am going to kill you!" Yasmine screams.

Lenelle blabs that she's the one that sent Osai the threatening text message from her backup cell phone. She confesses that she talked the maintenance man into letting her into Osai's house. She then installed a camera, in hopes of possibly capturing their affair.

Afterwards, she recorded and watched their sex acts from her cell phone.

Lenelle discloses that she never gave the cabbie a chance. Ramone is the only guy she dated, after she broke up with Osai, because he financially provided for her. Yasmine stares in shock.

"I stole a prescription pad from Osai's desk and wrote out prescriptions for mental medications in yo' name. The pharmacist loved me in my mini-sundress. He offered to fill the prescription for me, without id, if I let him rub my legs…and I did. Then, I began poisoning your lunch with the meds." Lenelle brags, proudly.

Yasmine begin to repeatedly spit on Lenelle. She grabs and restrains her.

"I'll hit you with this stun gun if you don't stop!" Lenelle threatens Yasmine.

Yasmine calms down.

Lenelle states that she never won a grocery gift card and that it was only a ploy to get her to eat her food, so she can mess her up.

"You are dead meat...bitch!" Yasmine hollers then spits in Lenelle's face.

"You will have nothing when you get out of here...that's if you do! Because, Osai is going to lose everything after I report him to the board. He won't be able to support you. You and I have identical handwriting, so no one can prove I wrote the prescriptions." Lenelle describes the plan.

Yasmine gets out of her bed and throws punches at Lenelle. She then grabs Yasmine's arm and twist it until she falls to the floor. Then, Lenelle rushes out of the room to the nurse's station and reports that Yasmine is a threat.

The nurse and Lenelle rush into her room. Yasmine begins to scream and curse. She grabs a glass, flower-filled vase from the nightstand and throws it at Lenelle and misses.

Another nurse hears the glass shatter and rushes to Yasmine's room and finds the nurse struggling to restrain her. She assist her coworker with placing a straitjacket on Yasmine. Lenelle smirks.

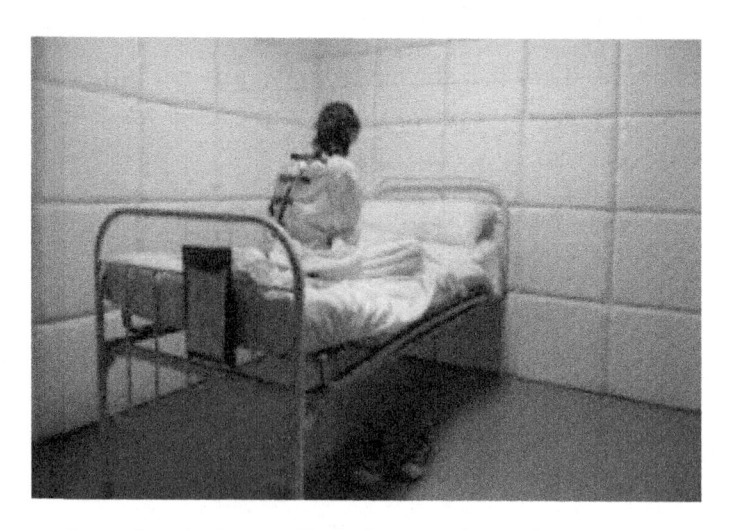

"I'll try to keep her in here a little longer since she's a danger to others." The nurse tells Lenelle.

"Thank you." Lenelle replies, happily, then exits the room.

"Hopefully she stays for life." Lenelle mumbles to herself.

"SHE'S LIVING HER DREAM"

A year later, Ramone and Yasmine's divorce finalizes. And, he marries Lenelle. Yasmine receives nothing from the split, because of committing adultery. Ramone has full custody of Deja because of Yasmine's incompetence.

The prolonged use of the psychiatric medicines causes Yasmine to have permanent, violent and uncontrollable muscle spasms. So, she's unable to care for herself. Therefore, she resides in a nursing home, where Lenelle is employed as a registered nurse.

Meanwhile, Lenelle exits the house to buy a bottle of wine for dinner.

She later returns then converse over dinner with her family.

"I'm glad you are my mama, now. My real mommy was too stuck up. You let me wear normal clothes and play outside. I hope mama never come back." Deja confesses to Lenelle.

"You do not talk about your mother that way. Now go to your room!" Ramone yells, uncorking the wine bottle.

Deja runs out of the dining area.

Lenelle and Ramone laugh at her comments.

"I can't believe you did your sister like that. I thought you were the trusting type." Ramone comments, passing the bottle of wine to Lenelle. "Thanks for exposing that whore. I had a feeling she was messing around when I saw the passion mark…that's why I started cheating, with only you." He tells, pouring dressing on his salad. "At least she got a hefty paycheck for it, instead of doing it for free." Ramone states.

"First of all, she's my stepsister…no blood relation." Lenelle responds, pouring herself a glass of wine.

"I got tested and I am so glad I didn't catch a disease from that thing." Ramone says, belittling Yasmine.

"Especially, the one you can't get rid of. Then, we would be messed up." Lenelle says, with mouthful of steak.

Ramone vents that he feels he may need some "happy pills" after learning of Yasmine's perfidious behavior.

"Most women have some whore in them, it takes something traumatic to bring it out." Lenelle schools.

"Well it has been proven that men are not the only dogs…women bark, too!" Ramone speaks, metaphorically, cutting his steak.

Lenelle and Ramone express their contentment with each other. Ramone pours himself a glass of wine, then they engage in a toast.

In addition, Osai lost his license to practice and is sentenced to 10 years in prison due to Lenelle reporting him.

An investigation revealed that Osai allowed Yasmine to write prescriptions for herself to support her drug habit, in exchange for sex. He has filed an appeal claiming he was not aware of Yasmine's actions. He is receiving no good luck and looks like he will be serving his full term, because no good attorney will take his case, due to a lack of funds.

Lenelle got Osai's bank account number from the check he wrote to Yasmine. She then had a man pose as Osai to enter the bank and withdraw all of his money. Osai has no clue of what happened to his funds.

Also, Kenise's divorce is final, so she has resigned from the gym and collects her alimony. She spends her spare time working at a charm school. It teaches teenage girls social grace and etiquette, so they will know to make their money in an honest manner, when they reach adulthood.

Jake was not reelected to judge and is now a divorce attorney. After his divorce, he still chased the skirts, which led to him stumbling up on his match.

He quickly fell in love with a stripper named Malaya. She is absolutely, exotically beautiful and from Brazil.

Jake quickly bought Malaya a $15,000 engagement ring. He nearly lost his mind when he learned from a friend that works at the airport, that she sold the ring and moved back to Brazil to be with her husband. Jake had no idea she was married.

He is now in therapy twice a week to get over his heartbreak. He has hired a private eye to track Malaya down, so he can sue her for the money he spent on the ring. So far, he has had no success, because the name "Malaya" is an alias.

The End

You may reach the author by sending correspondence to:

Tijuana Boswell

PO Box 3059

Memphis, Tn. 38173-0059

Email: tboswell73@yahoo.com

*Google the author's name to order copies of novel(s)

Made in the USA
Monee, IL
05 April 2021